Praise for Antonia Fraser

Must You Go?: My Life with Harold Pinter

"Combining disarming emotional frankness
with restrained elegance, Antonia Fraser
weaves her diary entries and memories into
a compelling and moving history of a long,
passionate relationship."
Katie Owen, *Sunday Times*

"[Written] with exemplary clarity and
courage … Fraser keeps her gaze steady and
her heart open."
Boyd Tonkin, *Independent*

"This book – full of funny and tender
things – satisfies on more than one level. It
is an intimate account of the life and habits
of a major artist; it is a pencil sketch of
British high society in the second half of the
twentieth century; and it is, more than either
of these things, and much more unusually,
a wonderfully full description of the deep
pleasures and comforts of married love."
Sam Leith, *Spectator*

"Unremittingly delicious: strange, rarefied, frequently hilarious."
Rachel Cooke, *Observer*

"It takes a daring biographer to turn her sharp eye on her own life as Antonia Fraser does so movingly and beautifully in her memoir."
Tina Brown, *Daily Beast*

≈

My History: A Memoir of Growing Up

"*My History*, a captivating memoir of her childhood and early youth … is a delight from start to finish. Antonia Fraser is warm, amusing, intelligent, generous and original. She says that her idea of perfect happiness is to be alone in a room with a house full of people. I can't think of a better way to start the year than to be alone in a room with this book."
Cressida Connolly, *Spectator*

"*My History* is a hugely enjoyable squishy romp, the literary equivalent of a big crumbling meringue at a society wedding."
Roger Lewis, *The Times*

"Fraser's previous volume of memoir, *Must You Go?*, an account of her life with Harold Pinter, was acclaimed as a moving love story. In this second instalment, she stands unabashed and alone – wise, self-deprecating and always entertaining."
Peter Stanford, *Daily Telegraph*

"Fraser's early years provide material as vivid and character-rich as her popular histories… Amiable and engaging as personal reminiscence, *My History* is also a sharp, unpretentious study of a writer in the making."
Wendy Smith, *Washington Post*

"A witty, perambulating memoir of youth and early adulthood… Nuanced and emotionally oblique in a most English fashion, [*My History*] offers a textured glimpse into a bygone era."
Publishers Weekly

"Engaging and elegiac."
Virginia Rounding, *Financial Times*

PATCHWORK PIECES

PATCHWORK PIECES

ANTONIA FRASER

FOR TRISTRAM

WITH LOVE

CONTENTS

Under the statue of Queen Elizabeth I
in Fleet Street, 2007.

PROLOGUE

WHEN I WAS a teenager I had a passion for patchwork. I liked the patterns, but even more than that I liked the action of creating the patchwork. There was something about pulling A to pieces, in order to create B, which I found infinitely satisfying. In a sense, this book satisfies that Passion for Patchwork. There is no particular order to the various pieces, and yet I hope that all together they make up a colourful picture of the history that I love, have loved and will always love.

1

90, HO!

THE CELEBRATION OF my 90th birthday came easily, like daily life. Or, actually, like daily life really is: sometimes easy, sometimes not. I had dinner with my son Orlando at Essenza and he suggested something about a summer lunch party at Bernhurst. I was just thinking that was quite a good idea when brother Thomas himself walked into the restaurant with Vanessa on his arm. I asked his permission. Without giving any impression of listening to what I had said, he granted it.

After that a lot depended on the sanctity of St Rebecca Fitzgerald, my daughter, who organised it all.

The important thing was to secure all my

descendants' presence. Thirty-two of them, of whom the last seven were great-grand-children, so probably not able to contribute more than plump pink faces (or, in the case of beloved Atticus, huge black eyes).

I decided to write a poem called 'Phew' to answer the speech son-in-law Edward Fitzgerald would undoubtedly make. (Easy rhyme with thirty-two.) And it was all going to work! Thirty-two descendants were due to be present, but then at the last minute came a call from Simon Soros.

Simon: Grandma, I can't come.
Me: This had better be good.
Simon: I've won the 'Funniest Person in Cincinnati' award.
Me: It is good.

But then granddaughter Eliza turned out to be pregnant with her fourth child, so the numbers added up once more. Phew!

The highlight of the feast was not a speech (or a poem), but a song. Grandson Billy snatched a microphone and roamed the tent singing: 'You make me feel so young.' He looked like a young god with his fair hair and fair face and the bonhomie that he carried with him.

The sun shone till evening and lingered even then.

Many old friends attended, such as Julian Sands and Jonathan Aitken, and Rebecca and I decided there would largely be no placement, which worked well.

Nothing was deliberate, for example Ronke was there because I truly love her, not because my brother Kevin brought her into my life. From the first we enjoyed each other's jokes: 'Has my sister arrived?' … then watching the bafflement creep across faces all around.

With Julian Sands and Jonathan Aitken.

2

32, PHEW

Hello my 32 Descendants
The magic number 32
Applies to you and you and you…
It actually applies to me as well as you
Born in 1932
So 32: you and me too
Phew
I can honestly assure you
That it's absolutely fine to
Be 90
A lot of time needed to pass
But I've got there at last
It remains to wish you all
The luck of reaching 90 too
That would be quite a Ball
Phew!

With George Weidenfeld and my mother, 1969.

3

ODDJOBS

SHORTLY AFTER I went to work for George Weidenfeld, I was compelled to write a book. It turned out to be extremely good training. I use the word 'compelled' deliberately, because it wasn't a book that I would have chosen to write. It was, in fact, a children's book.

What happened was this. George swept into the Weidenfeld & Nicolson board meeting, following his regular session with the directors of Marks & Spencer, at which a list of children's classics for the next few months was decided. We would then illustrate them, finding exciting modern illustrators, publish as a new edition and sell to M&S, to our entire profit, since classics obviously paid no royalties.

On this occasion the list included *King Arthur and the Knights of the Round Table.* I saw my chance.

'That won't do, George,' I said importantly. 'T. H. White is still in copyright…'

'Then you Antonia will write it,' replied George, without a pause, turning to the next book. I gasped. It was Nicolas Thompson, my co-editor, who pointed out that I would actually be paid more or less – if not exactly – what Malory had got five hundred years before. Anyway, I wrote the book, received that modest sum of £100 one-off payment (absolutely no royalties) and was published for the first time throughout Marks & Spencer at the age of twenty-two.

After this prodigious triumph – as I saw it – I naturally followed it up the next year with *Robin Hood.* When the choice was made known, I smiled complacently. Who else but me could take on this wild adventure story? But the fact was that with Robin, not Arthur, there was a problem of plot. A Malory did not exist: with Vol. II, I had to be my own Malory. Fortunately, the spirit of the detective story writer was beginning to burn in me, and with the invention of a character called Black Barbara I soon felt I was well away.

My next two published works were of a very different ilk.

Dolls and *The History of Toys* were probably good practice for writing to order, and even better practice for researching. I remember being intoxicated by the history of Queen Mary's dolls' house, and then learning how the working classes would use saucepans and spoons to fashion imaginative toys.

With Tony Gould-Davies of
the Book Club Associates, 1974.

4

STARRY SKIES

'LIKE ME, YOU'RE a Virgo,' said Sonia Orwell. 'And so is George.' At that point I had no idea what she was talking about. A North Oxford education, to say nothing of the convent follow-up, had simply not touched on the language of the stars. I remembered going to a bazaar with Grannie and allowing my palm to be read but I can't remember any of the prophecies, only that Grannie (Katie Chamberlain, a keen Unitarian) became extremely cross, first with the palmist, then with me.

'Rubbish,' she declared firmly. 'Say after me: "This is all rubbish."'

But the stars? At that point I had been

working for George Weidenfeld at his publishing company for about a year; we had recently been joined by the voluptuous Sonia, widow of George Orwell, and the toast of literary London. Her long blonde hair swept into the office rather late most mornings. She then regaled me with tales of her doings the night before, generally studded with glamorous artists' names, such as Lucian Freud and Francis Bacon.

'George and I have decided to take you with us to see the latest astrologer,' continued Sonia. She gave a wonderfully starry name and an address in Mayfair.

'Three Virgos,' said the astrologer, and Sonia nodded vigorously. By now I had recovered from the shock of finding that I had apparently returned to the Virgoan state in which I had been born. I had read up a little on the stars and discovered to my surprise that Little Miss Virgo was prim and demure and ultra tidy… This description did not seem to fit George Weidenfeld any more than it fitted Sonia (or me). So it was with genuine curiosity that I had accompanied George and Sonia to the large mansion block in Mayfair, inhabited by the lady whom I shall call Madam Astra. She proved to be an extremely neat middle-aged lady, civil and apparently warm-hearted, since she greeted me personally with enthusiasm.

'Alethea, your chart is so interesting,' she assured me. Vanity told me to accept the compliment and not point out that my name was actually not Alethea, but Antonia.

'I see books, lots of books…' and she proceeded to embroider this theme. I was slightly surprised. It was true that I had published *King Arthur and the Knights of the Round Table*, in the Heirloom Library.

'What about babies?' I asked. My best friend Lucy had just given birth to her first child and I was rather jealous.

'No,' said Madam Astra. 'No babies. I don't see any babies.' I felt one big pang of disappointment before being swept by a mighty resolution.

Yes. There would be babies. Whatever the stars said. Later, as the mother of six, I told the story to Lucy.

'Well,' she said kindly, 'She was fifty per cent right, wasn't she?'

≈

The stars twinkled again brightly in the sky during the precious years of my friendship with the American novelist Alison Lurie. I realised later that Alison had, in her amusing way, used a knowledge of astrology as an entry into literary London. That, combined with wit, charm and a series of brilliant novels, made her a most popular candidate for dinner parties.

Now I was not only Virgo – no one was, apparently, ruled by a *single* sign – but also heavily involved with Cancer and the Moon, with Cancer rising and the Moon trailing its silver tracks everywhere. Thank goodness that I could stop feeling prim and demure and take up sensitivity in a big way.

About this time came the famous first encounter with Harold, which much later I shared with the world in *Must You Go?* When Alison first looked at my horoscope – in response to my own excited request – she frowned and bowed her face. Alison had beautiful dark red hair; now, some kind of similarly coloured blush seemed to seize her.

She started to babble; at the end of our meeting she asked herself for lunch and later became a familiar and welcome visitor in Scotland. It was many years later, when Harold and I had been happily married for a decade, that she told me what had happened. She had seen in my chart a hideous scandal! And hadn't felt capable of telling me about it. She decided to support me with her friendship… As she certainly did throughout the years before Harold and I managed to bring about our felicitous marriage.

Once the truth was out, I was sufficiently curious about my chart to ask for details.

Alison pointed to the conjunction with Jupiter, which promised all these things.

I took a quick decision never to have my horoscope delineated again – it could not get better, it could only get worse.

Anne Boleyn.

5

THE UGLY ONE

WHEN I FIRST had the idea of writing about the six wives of Henry VIII, I got in a muddle. That is to say, I got the wives in a muddle, something Henry VIII was also known to do, although in rather a different way.

What happened was this. I was driving along a Sussex lane with my husband Harold when I suddenly saw a notice saying 'Hever Castle'. Harold was unimpressed, as he had come to the conclusion (he told me later) that Sussex had rather too many castles for its own good. But as I was at the wheel I was able to park and wheel us in for a good tour without too many complaints from Harold, or from the other tourists who were mainly school children at that time of day. After all, Anne of Cleves, who lived at Hever, was one of the famous six… I was immediately excited.

As we proceeded down the narrow corridors stuffed with pictures, I spent more time reading the captions than admiring the stuffy little faces squished under caps and crowns. Imagine my delight when I read the caption *Anne of Cleves*! The historic hostess of the castle herself. Closely followed by *Anne Boleyn.*

I was studying Anne Boleyn, admiring her neat prettiness, when I heard a young male voice at my elbow: 'There she is, there she is, the ugly one.' There were other voices, all young males it seemed, and the word 'ugly' seemed to be endlessly repeated. Ugly? Who was ugly round here? It was the jolting of an elbow and the jostle of a shoulder which gave me the clue.

In other words, there had been a mistake, a huge error. Seductive Anne Boleyn had been mistaken for ultra-plain Anne of Cleves.

Once the wrong name had been attached, in the imagination of the boy spectator it was easy to follow on. Anne Boleyn was now terribly ugly and Anne of Cleves was fearfully pretty. Wasn't she? And, curiously enough, as I stood there in the castle I began to see the delightful Anne Boleyn through different eyes; she began to look ugly, and uglier…

Hastily I withdrew. But I had learnt my lesson. Behind the Scenes of History everyone was beautiful and everyone was ugly according to very different standards. I was going to have to find out what these standards were.

'Cricket is just the same,' said Harold hospitably, when I confided the Ugly Anne problem to him later. I realised that it was a sort of compliment and smiled in what I hoped was a Boleynesque fashion.

Thereafter I spent a great deal of time trying to edit my ideas of beauty in accordance with those of the time. Was Mary Queen of Scots really the most beautiful princess, as pronounced by the whole of Europe? The important fact here was that they believed it and acted as if it were true. Even John Knox had compliments to pay, no charmer he. 'Pleasing' was how he described her, and recorded that the people of Edinburgh called out 'God bless that sweet face' as she went on her way. Brantôme and Ronsard both praised in particular her sweet voice when she spoke at the opening of Parliament: '*VOX DIANAE! The Voice of a Goddess*'. Brantôme picked out the exquisite whiteness of her skin and compared it with the whiteness of her veil when she was in mourning. The poet Chastelard fell hysterically in love with her. It was actually the Venetian Ambassador who pronounced her, 'personally the most beautiful in Europe'.

Yet when I came, surreptitiously as it were, to examine her looks insofar as I was able, I realised how much of it was based on fame and legend, how comparatively little on actual beauty. Her outstanding feature was her height: probably about 5' 11" – that is, really tall in an age when average heights were much lower than they are today. On the other hand, she was in no way beefy: she had the delicacy of her mother Mary of Guise. At the same time her height must have mattered to her – when dancing, for example, and I became quickly convinced that the early love of Mary for her husband Henry, Lord Darnley was rooted in their matching heights. Although I muttered these thoughts to myself in the British Library, I was aware that I had been a tall teenager… I could remember the embarrassment of dancing with boys shorter than myself. At the same time there was a vivid memory of discovering a tall handsome young Scottish baronet (whatever happened to him?).

But I understood Mary's love for Darnley in a way that was quite different from his important position in the Scottish royal succession. Both loves could exist, and exist at the same time: worldly and romantic; but where Mary Queen of Scots was concerned, I never forget that image of a lily-white princess, towering over most of the nobility of her court. Whereas the image of Ugly Anne had taught me something suddenly and sharply, Mary had an element of a fairy princess: and it was up to me to recreate the idea of the beautiful for my readers – whether at the court of Louis XIV or Charles II or later George III.

One of the first persons I had to convince was myself, but once I had done it there was no going back. I throw the name of Anne Boleyn quite happily into the flowery marsh of my imagination and out comes a delightful image. That goes for the opposite sex too, of course. The physical appearance of Henry VIII was quite as important in historical terms, if you think about it, as that of the tasty Anne Boleyn. A slim and handsome prince is transformed by age and injury into a hefty disabled lump…

At this point I asked myself exactly how I could know the dimensions of Henry the Lump. And at this point also occurred one of those coincidences that make a happy marriage blessed. For Harold was invited to take his beloved cricket team to Leeds (not Lord's), and there by coincidence were the Royal Armouries, transferred from the Tower of London. Few tourists, I imagine, arrive there politely asking if they might try on the armour of Henry VIII. The man in charge – I was about to say the jailer – was possessed of splendid calm.

'You can't do that,' he said. 'But you can try on his horse's armour if you like.'

Two things happened next. I immersed myself in a huge horse's head and, at the same time, a large school party arrived. They greeted the sight of the mythical horse with hoots and shrieks and cries of 'Me too'. I can't say that I derived much wisdom from peering out of the eye holes of the metal headpiece, but I did get the message: armour made you the centre of attention, which I am sure was just as true in the sixteenth century as in the twenty-first.

The Duke of Monmouth.

6

MARRYING THE
MOTHER

ONE OF THE important aspects of my trying to write history was that I began to view quite ordinary situations in a different light. Why should the youthful Charles II bother about children, his own or anyone else's? When his father was executed by Parliament in 1649, Charles II, as he became, was not yet nineteen. Time surely to be concentrating on his own youth rather than the youth of the country. The young prince in exile was a handsome man with the darkly attractive looks of his Medici ancestors. He would not lack for little friends, whether they were princesses or chambermaids.

But of course, the real question that occupied Europe after the death of Charles I was not so much the little prince or princess playing in the royal nursery as the fine lady who might be seated on the royal throne beside her husband: in short, who would be the Queen and so the mother of the future restored dynasty. And what mattered about this fine lady was, first, that she should be properly married and secondly that she should give birth to an heir (preferably but not essentially male).

Very early on, the future Charles II began to demonstrate that male infertility was never going to be one of his problems. At the same time, it became uncomfortably obvious that marrying the mother of the future monarch was another matter altogether. That is, to marry someone of suitably royal blood, able to bear healthy children, preferably male, and bringing with them perhaps a royal alliance or two. Compared to a light-hearted evening in a great hall, ending perhaps in a sweet little memento nine months later – the former was an infinitely harder task.

All of this was in considerable contrast to my own life: by this time, I had two children and was expecting a third. No question here of succession to anything! Just a rather anguished listing of expenses at my monthly accounting and muttered sentences like: 'If we have a boy [we already had two daughters] public schools are getting to be terrifying in how much they cost…' This would be followed by a resolute promise to myself: 'Enough. I shall think about Charles II and his future, not my own.' And I buried myself in the anguishing but highly enjoyable history of Europe and Charles, telling myself to concentrate on the English Succession and forget about the cost of a British taxi ride.

As Charles the exile wandered round Europe, the first possible future monarch made his appearance. He would be known as the Duke of Monmouth, but at this stage he was simply the delightful baby son of a saucy

Welsh girl. It was at the Hague that Charles first encountered Lucy Walter, whom John Evelyn described as 'brown and beautiful, bold but insipid'. Now he found her again, and the couple in a manner of speaking fell in love, at any rate were linked by enough passion for there to be rumours of a marriage. And there were enough rumours for the boy known as Monmouth to be thought to have a real claim to the throne – at a time when Charles II was sinking fast towards the grave. It was all a question of marriage. Plenty of girls existed with whom King Charles had had loving relationships, but could any of them conceivably claim to be his wife – and thus the mother of a legitimate prince?

Although there was some contemporary doubt about Monmouth's paternity, and rumours about Robert Sidney (with whom Lucy Walter certainly had a fling), in fact his strong appearance clearly echoes that of Charles II. The real question was that of legit-imacy: in short, whether Lucy Walter could claim the role once occupied by Henrietta Maria.

It is interesting to reflect how often in English – and Scottish and Irish – history, the identity of the mother, as well as that of the father, has a special importance. In fact, it was while studying Charles II in the 1970s that I discovered my own by-no-means-unique royal descent. In short, this sprang from Barbara Villiers, one of Charles' principal mistresses. The importance of Barbara lay in the length of time she exercised her power over the King. One of her sons – named Fitzroy, that is the King's son – ended up being created Duke of Grafton, and a huge proportion of the English aristocracy can claim descent from him, including the late Diana Princess of Wales (and thus by further descent our future King). My finest hour came when I was invited to go to Edinburgh to celebrate the anniversary of the Royal College of Physicians, founded by Charles II. I decided to begin by claiming boldly: 'Both you and I…' surveying the crowded hall 'can claim descent from King Charles II.'

To return happily and less boastfully to the seventeenth century and the true royal succession, it ended as it had begun – with a tricky situation. People had worried away about the succession to the unmarried virgin Queen Elizabeth I, a worry which had ended with the emergence of James VI from Scotland, to be enshrined as James VI and I of Scotland and England. With James II on the throne, the situation grew even more complicated. Who was to be the next monarch? The question of the mother emerged again. Would the succession fall to the Protestant princess, Anne, daughter of the royal lady in waiting and the first wife of James II? Or was it to be the baby son of the Catholic second wife?

The bridge where Cromwell planned
the Battle of Preston.

7

OPTICAL RESEARCH

(1)

Wᴡʜᴇɴ I ᴛᴏʟᴅ my accountant that I was busy with my 'Optical Research', I spoke nothing but the truth. Although it would have been possible to phrase it somewhat differently. I could have described myself as 'going places' – Stirling Castle comes to mind, where Mary Queen of Scots was born – and looking at them. Not so glamorous, perhaps, but frankly the essence of Optical Research.

Ever since I read *Our Island Story* as a child, I have always wanted to visit historic places. During the harsh winter of 1940, when I reached one particular chapter, all of Oxford, where I lived, seemed shrouded in ice and snow. At this point I read about the escape of Queen Matilda across the ice surrounding Oxford Castle. It took no feat of imagination to recreate her flight: I, Antonia Pakenham, in my gym shoes and dungarees, might not resemble Queen Matilda, but my internal spirit was just the same.

Of course, Optical Research became of maximum importance when it was a question of a battlefield.

My second book, following the unexpected success of *Mary Queen of Scots*, was about Oliver Cromwell, under the title of *Cromwell, Our Chief of Men*. The line was taken from Milton, which I thought gave the whole enterprise a note of class:

Cromwell, our chief of men, who through a
  cloud
Not of war only, but detractions rude
Guided by faith and matchless fortitude,
To peace and truth thy glorious way hast
  ploughed.

Quoting Milton was all very well, but immediately I encountered the problem of warfare and tactics in general, a real issue for a girl who had not been old enough in the War (unlike our late beloved Queen) to drive an army vehicle.

Luckily, in a happy contrast of characters, my two marriages, twenty-five years apart, each produced some valuable information essential to the plot. It was very important to me that my first husband had fought in the War and was able to apply his intelligence to the whole question of Optical Research from the point of view of the twentieth century.

In fact, I had plenty of good optical advice available because my second husband, Harold Pinter, was cricket mad and, in my opinion if not his own, frequently applied the rules of twenty-first-century cricket to the rules of seventeenth-century warfare with success. He also had a healthy appreciation of midland landscape and frequently stopped the car to admire some vast green field, only to discover to his delight that it contained an active cricket match.

Scottish castles, in fact castles in general, provided some lovely glimpses of how history had come to be made. There was something about a turret, and the twisting staircase which came with it, which I found infinitely exciting. This feeling rose to its heights with Fotheringhay Castle, where poor Mary had finally been executed on the orders of her cousin Queen Elizabeth at the age of forty-four.

Berlin, 1989.

8

OPTICAL RESEARCH
(2)

WHEN I STUDIED Irish internal politics I had a very happy time – and a very surprising one. My niece Eliza had done wonders with the family archive. She was just what was needed: intelligent, amusing and knowledgeable. She gave new life to family characters and I began to find them living in my mind, or rather myself living in their world.

I took a particular fancy to 'Brunswick Tom', as I persisted in calling Thomas, Earl of Longford, my ancestor, not for his liberal politics – rather the reverse – but for his dashing individual spirit. I used to gaze at his picture in the stately Tullynally dining room. Tullynally was the home of the Longfords, originally known as Pakenham Hall and rechristened by my brother Thomas.

I would metaphorically wag my finger at him: 'We Catholics are coming to get you,' I promised. On Sundays going to Mass, as I did, in Castlepollard, I looked across at the Protestant church and thought how it could all have been different. Thank St Patrick and St Bridget it wasn't. The order of conversion in my family was first my father, then my mother and finally Thomas my brother and me. Our younger brother and sisters were born Catholics.

At one point I even thought of writing a study of Northern Ireland and the Orange troubles: in fact, the last year of my father's life led to a wonderful relationship between us as he discussed growing up a Protestant in Catholic Ireland.

The subject, however, would have been a study of Northern Irish history, including William III, James II and Louis XIV – and of these I liked only Louis XIV, so I took myself off and very happily wrote a study called *Love and Louis XIV* (summed up by one reviewer as 'Sex and Politics in two languages').

SAVE THE DATE!

A Celebration of Dragon Women
with guest speaker
Lady Antonia Fraser (OD 1944)

Saturday 12th April 2008
Reception and Lunch from 11.30am

Further details and booking form will follow shortly
01865 315415 or ods@dragonschool.org

9

THE DRAGON AND
DUNSANY

'THE ENEMY DOESN'T come out in the day,' said our mother conversationally, with the air of one announcing that the *Daily Herald* had not arrived.

Just as well, I thought, as I packed my Dragon bag with the *Dragon Book of Verse* in order to occupy myself during the long journey to Dublin. *The Dragon Book of Verse* was the anthology issued by my school, and it had a magic touch: however many times you read it, you could always find a ballad or a sonnet which you adored and which you had never read before.

The Dragon School was the first big

adventure of my life. Here were three hundred boys and thirty girls – or was it four hundred and forty? What did the precise figure matter? The fact was that the Dragon was a boys' prep school and a few, a very few, girls were admitted. In theory they were the sisters of older Dragons, but too many questions were never asked at the Dragon (it was one of the strengths of the school). The fact was that once you were a She Dragon you belonged forever to a sacred race. You learned Latin, you learned Greek, you learned difficult Maths, you learned impossible poetry, you starred in Shakespeare plays. I'll stop there and remember how wonderful it was to know that every year you would have the best part in the Shakespeare play just because you were a girl.

The summit of my career, played in my last year when I was verging on twelve years old, was Lady Macbeth. I shall never forget that summer term.

'Unsex me now…' I demanded of the entire Upper School.

The producer, J. B. Brown, always known as 'Bruno', showed clear signs of favouritism and I was his favourite. Never mind my lack of any singing voice, in the yearly Gilbert and Sullivan I was given some paltry role. Bruno used to come on stage and put his ear low, beneath the ardently singing mouth of the child on stage. When in time he leant beneath me, and listened, he paused and then simply said: 'Don't.'

That was one reverse which I didn't mind at all. I never thought I could sing. The next reverse was a real humiliation and taught me that favouritism is like tissue paper: it tears very easily. The previous school play had been *Twelfth Night*, and I had of course given a brilliant Viola. Then Bruno announced that this year's Shakespeare was to be *As You Like It*. 'And you, Antonia, will play Celia.'

I walked home happily down Chadlington Road, confiding to my many friends I encountered on the way: 'Our Shakespeare this term is *As You Like It* and I am starring as Celia.' It was my best friend Felicity

Wilding, out of a sense of accuracy I still believe, rather than a wish to snub, who pointed out: 'Actually, the star of the play is called Rosalind. And she is being played by Scilla Hett.'

I rushed to the text. It was true. I realised that Bruno had fallen in love again, and Scilla Hett was now the petted favourite. My heart was broken.

Under the circumstances, a trip to Ireland seemed a welcome distraction, an opportunity to think about shamrocks and elves and nymphs and forget about the Dragon.

So Thomas and I set out for the journey lasting, it seemed, about a day. It was wartime, and we crossed the Irish Sea, but somehow we were not frightened. We ended with the wonderful unrationed food (i.e. sweets) of Dublin's fair city.

'Uncle Edward wants to give Thomas something,' said our Nanny, carelessly. We imagined for some extraordinary reason a silk shirt. It was actually a castle and a large estate, since Aunt Christine and Uncle

Edward had no children; our father was Edward's younger brother.

On our way we stayed with our Great Aunt and Uncle, Beatrice and Eddie. Uncle Eddie – Lord Dunsany – was a famous playwright and poet and, apart from that, an extremely eccentric man whom Aunt Beatrice desperately tried to control by crying out: 'Pony, pony, there are ladies present…'

But once we children were installed at Dunsany, it was all bliss. There seemed to be four square meals a day (breakfast and tea both being substantial, with plenty of that precious meat so seldom seen in England). What was more, I inspired Dunsany the poet who wrote 'Lines to Antonia' and had them published in *Punch*. This would have caused me to smirk in dentists' waiting rooms if I had been lucky enough to get there. Unfortunately, my large merry teeth never seemed to have anything wrong with them demanding something as expensive as a dentist. So, I had to take the word of fellow Dragons for the entry in *Punch*.

In short, I fell in love with Ireland at the age of twelve. I responded to this love by announcing – to myself – that I was Anglo-Irish, a nationality which enabled me to choose any fragment of English and Irish and weave it together. Once I was married to Hugh Fraser, proud member of a Highland clan, there was more to add. Surely someone who wrote as Antonia Fraser and had an Inverness-shire home was actually Scottish? Or, as I overheard one of my children saying at a party, 'I am half Scottish, half English and half Irish.' Which said more for her patriotism than her maths.

THE
WEAKER
VESSEL

Woman's lot in seventeenth-century England

ANTONIA FRASER

10

MANY LIVES MAKE
LIFE WORK

Travelling in a train to Birmingham in the seventies I read a life-changing work. This was *Religion and the Decline of Magic* by Keith Thomas.

I won't pretend that the whole of my subsequent study of women in the seventeenth century, *The Weaker Vessel: Woman's Lot in Seventeenth-Century England*, sprang out of my typewriter fully formed. The book was not published till 1984. But then, the great change Thomas had wrought in my attitude to biography was fully acknowledged; in England *The Weaker Vessel* received the premier history prize. In the U.S., spurred on by me praising myself on lecture tour, it became a most unlikely bestseller.

What Keith Thomas had done in his brilliant book changed my whole attitude to biography. I would always feel at my happiest falling in love, as it were, with a single person, but now I saw that there could be another kind of work well worth doing. In other words, Many Lives Make Life Work – or, anyway, create extremely valuable worlds against which heroes and heroines (and saints and villains) can flourish, instead of focusing on a single person, as in a biography.

In the course of my researches I began to pine after writing a book about women fighting – that is, fighting in the Civil War. Interestingly, some of the soldiers turned out to be African, as some Elizabethan courtiers had been. The fact was that, in many villages, the disappearance of the alpha male to war left a great deal of muscle-grinding work to do for the surviving head of the household, the woman. And the fact was that these muscles were in any case marvellously developed.

When the women stripped off to wash in the army it was only their lack of the particular male characteristics which gave the game away: shoulders, arms, hands, thighs were all highly masculine at first quick glance. But there was one danger and that faced almost every female soldier ... pregnancy. This was an age when contraception was in its infancy. Yes, Roman soldiers had indeed left objects made of goatskin behind them, some of the more sophisticated relics. There had been little progress since.

I still haven't managed to write that book, or inspire anyone else to do so. But in the meantime I have taken a happy interest in composite female books.

In 1984 I had the honour of starting up the Authors' Foundation, suggested by Mark Le Fanu, together with the most distinguished contemporary biographer Michael Holroyd. It was intended to give grants to deserving authors in order for them to write specific works, and to mark the 100th anniversary of the Society of Authors. After thirty years I gave up alternate chairing, but left behind an Antonia Fraser Grant, which was for a book centred on a woman – or women.

Maybe one day there will come a request for support while writing a composite work about women fighting. In my mild way, I am fiercely keen on it!

Happy Birthday Antonia

1977

11

LOST CHILDREN

I CALL THEM my *lost children* – the bio-graphical subjects where I duly fell in love but then fell smartly out of love again. Being then, in three cases, left with an unfulfilled and in my opinion unfulfillable contract.

Most notable was of course Queen Elizabeth I. After I wrote *Mary Queen of Scots* it seemed that many of my readers had only one ambition, which was to read a study of Queen Bess by the recent winner with Queen Mary.

I also discovered (twice) that the mere con-junction of the names Queen Elizabeth and Antonia Fraser provoked mention of large sums of money.

'Hooray,' I murmured, at the mention

of so many noughts by my agreeable agent Jonathan.

And I started work. The trouble was that I was like a barrister employed by the other side. Every time there was a notional confrontation of the two ladies, I found myself arguing at length and, for me, most plausibly, for Queen Mary.

Then it got worse. I started to get angry, first of all with Robert Cecil and then with Elizabeth herself. With sinking heart I realised that anger gets nothing done in the world of biography. Why hadn't I faced the fact that I was still in love with Mary Queen of Scots. It was a terrible decision, but I decided to return the money. Christmas was fairly grim that year.

The second mistake was less serious (and less money). I simply took a fancy to the idea of Queen Alexandra, Danish wife of King Edward VII. But each book I read convinced me all over again that the reason she was so little known in history was because there was so little to know.

It was left to the third case to provide the greatest distraction and, at the same time, the most enjoyable experience.

This was to be a study of the Battle of the Boyne in July 1690, where the Protestant William III fought and defeated the Catholic Louis XIV; thus Protestant Ireland was established. Protestant Ireland was the country in which my father was brought up (he was a Catholic convert in 1940). 2000, the year in which I worked hard on the book, turned out to be the last year of his productive life – he died at ninety-five. I spent most of that year travelling to Ireland, and when I got there talking to my father about what it meant to grow up a Protestant in a Catholic country. Both in terms of History and in terms of our relationship, these were experiences I would never have had without attempting that book.

The fact that I gradually realised I would never understand ancient Ireland sufficiently to write about it didn't matter. I had had that precious year in which – he in his nineties and me in my seventies – I got to know my beloved father.

I repaid that money too, feeling that I had learnt a lot. And also feeling deeply grateful for having done so. This lost child waves at me from the headlines of the Irish newspapers – and I wave happily back.

12

ENCORE

I NEVER EXPECTED to find myself considering the subject of male impotence while
researching in the archives. Then the extraordinary chance took place whereby I found
myself, first of all, sitting at a cricket match
in Berkshire and discussing the subject, then
plunging into further research at the British
Library.

It all began with poor Marie Antoinette,
sent away from Austria to France far too
young. The wedding night of two teenagers
– the future Louis XVI and Marie Antoinette
– was witnessed by savage courtiers and
found distinctly wanting.

Naturally I had to probe the unfortunate

failure of the young Louis and consider the various theories which might explain it.

Was it in fact the fault of Marie Antoinette, which seemed a bit unfair considering her extreme youth? Or was it, as was far more likely, the failure of the royal French bridegroom? Louis happened to leave behind various traces of medical trouble, carrying with them the possibility of serious infection. It was at this point that the word 'phimosis' crossed my path. That is to say, one morning in the British Library I read of the possibility that Louis was a sufferer. In the afternoon, at a cricket match, I sat next to an agreeable doctor who happened to be an expert in the subject. An appointment followed. It became quickly apparent for various reasons that phimosis was not Louis XVI's problem.

Good for cricket!

The next step was to consider that, if phimosis were not the culprit – basically his diary revealed an athleticism that did not fit chronologically with his alleged infection – what was?

This took longer, but in the end I reached the stage, following the young Queen's career, of understanding that the young couple were both psychologically wounded in that respect. And the day finally came when the King made it. And the Queen lay back in her beautiful bed at Versailles and said 'Encore!'

At least, I'm sure she must have said something like that.

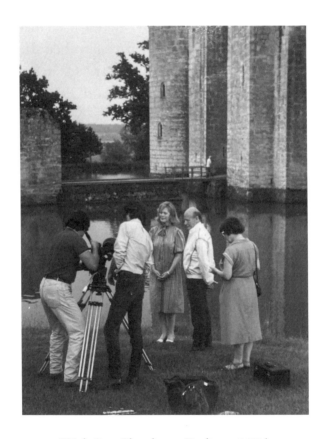

With Roy Plomley at Bodiam, 1984.

13

CATHOLIC DETERMINATION

I F IT'S IMPORTANT to convey beauty then it is equally important (and arguably rather more fun) to convey the ugly side of life. In other words, wickedness. But of course, it is perfectly possible that your wicked is my wonderful, and that in the wild terrain of wicked plots a profound disagreement can exist not only between the plotters at the time but between historians and other commentators ever since.

The Gunpowder Plot of 1605 is a perfect example of this.

As a Protestant child (I was converted to Catholicism, following my mother, when I was thirteen) I thought I knew everything about the Gunpowder Plot. As a passionate Catholic I tried to persuade people not to burn or torture Guy Fawkes: although it could be tricky in wartime, when almost everything seemed worthy of being pitched into the flames. My conversion to Catholicism changed the emphasis entirely. I was now on the side of the Catholic plotters – but wait! What plotters? Were there in fact any plotters, or was the whole conspiracy a nasty English Protestant invention?

The story of the Gunpowder Plot taught me a valuable historical lesson about wickedness. Once you accepted the wickedness of the Plot itself, where frankly the plan was to murder a great number of the House of Lords by blowing them up, then one line of analysis was to infer that the aims of the Plot were themselves noble, justifying such awful means for a righteous end. The alternative was rather unpleasant: it meant accepting the fact that a lot of very nasty people had deliberately planned a terrible crime, of which murder by bombing was the simplest part. These nasty people were incidentally Catholics.

It was much easier for me to relate sympathetically to the intense Catholic problems in Jacobean England, and then suggest the solution that might have been planned by the hard-pressed Catholics at the time.

One such solution was a conspiracy to do away with the powerful Protestant forces by planning their demolition.

At this point I found myself investigating a variety of things not in general use (anyway, not in my household) such as gunpowder and its staying power. How long can you leave a pile of gunpowder mouldering in a stone tower and expect it to do its duty at the end? There are other easier questions: who has easy access to gunpowder in the first place?

All this was essential research before the important ins and outs of Catholic and Protestant character were reached.

It took me to some weird places. My

favourite place was definitely the archives at
Farm Street Catholic Church, conveniently
situated opposite the Connaught Hotel.
Because it lay beneath the church, the
lighting seemed to me to come out of a novel
by Harrison Ainsworth, as the slim dark
figures of priests and monks passed silently to
and fro. There was definitely an otherworldly
feel to it all. My favourite priest – he was a
keen student of the Plot – was Father Francis
Edwards S.J. Unfortunately, Father Francis
and I disagreed about the Plot itself: his
analysis of the plot was that it was something
invented by courtiers to smirch the Catholic
reputation; mine was a real plot born out of
desperation. All the same, we became great
friends. Years later, going sadly to his funeral
at Farm Street, I reflected that Father Francis,
now all-seeing in heaven, must know the final
truth of the whole affair. I then sat up with a
jolt and thought: 'Perhaps he had been right
all along, and now confirmed in his view.'

In complete contrast to the Gunpowder
Plot, I later chose to study a subject which I

have chosen to call Catholic Determination, but more generally is known as Catholic Emancipation. The late great figure of justice Jeremy Hutchinson, informed of my new subject at a noisy party towards the end of his life, mistook Catholic Emancipation, with considerable amusement, for the less appropriate subject of Catholic Masturbation.

I thought it was important to demonstrate that Catholicism was in fact a highly inclusive religion, in spite of being criminally against the law and punishable by hideous tortures as well as outright executions.

I believe that my own Catholic 'history' (of conversion) was helpful here. I had been to both Protestant and Catholic schools and in my head carried a little private history of Catholicism in England. This did not encourage me to believe in the punishment of anyone for religious reasons. Admittedly I found Catholic Determination, when violently expressed by the Gunpowder Plot, definitely exciting. But equally fascinating were topics like the influence of nuns and convents on women's education.

My heroine was a certain Mary Ward, a nun, from an old Catholic family, who, when things got very difficult for Catholics in England, went abroad and founded a new order. 'In time women shall do much' was her watchword, and as a thirteen-year-old I secretly adopted it as mine. To my absolute delight I found that Blessed Mary Ward I.B.V.M. (Institute of the Blessed Virgin Mary) was the patron of St Mary's Ascot, the school to which I was sent to acquire Catholic Determination. It was Mary Ward who asked the Pope to let her found an Order of English Virgins. Her sovereign belief in women's education linked her pleasantly to my own mother: although my mother was granted only four young women to educate, in the shape of her daughters, and Mary Ward flourished not only in her lifetime but in multiple schools and orders thereafter.

I found studying Catholic Emancipation (*sic.* Jeremy) enormously pleasurable. I think the two political subjects I had studied following my two memoirs, *Must You Go?* and *My History*, had prepared me for it. Not only did I have a story to tell, but I could feel inspired to tell it. Some of the things which happened to the Catholics before Emancipation made my flesh creep with their dark violence. But here I came – I came with a solution. At the end of my book, people voted, including in Ireland and – hoorah! My hero Daniel O'Connell (he was very much part of the solution) had won a seat in the British House of Commons.

In fact, the law had a role in all my last books, including my study of Caroline Norton, to which title I added 'The Case of the Married Woman' – a nineteenth-century heroine who wished to see justice for women.

Tullynally Castle.

14

OLIVER CRUMBLE

IN THE NURSERY he was generally known as Oliver Crumble, that is, a rather foolish figure who would show signs of weakness at any given moment. Yet, as has been noted, when I came to choose the title of my biography after working on the subject for five years during the seventies, I selected *Cromwell, Our Chief of Men*. This was the opening of Milton's stately poem, and there was no doubt that Cromwell had moved from a nursery joke to the lord of all as a direct result of my researches.

Actually, the choice of Cromwell as a subject had come as a great surprise to a number of people, including myself, after the success of *Mary Queen of Scots* in 1969. It has been mentioned that recommendations from my readers were headed by Elizabeth I, followed by Bonnie Prince Charlie. The latter and his whole period would actually be brilliantly covered by a member of my family in a way that I could admire but not possibly emulate. Queen Elizabeth was different. Two or three times I felt I had something special to say and accepted a contract: then the special thing, whatever it was, wandered away in favour of private favourites such as the daily life of English women in the Civil War.

The Weaker Vessel struck me as an appropriate title, even though the brilliant – and brilliantly polite – Claire Tomalin exclaimed on the subject of my new book: '*A week with Ethel!* That is an interesting title.'

Fortunately, whatever Claire imagined was shared by the public and Ethel went on to win a Wolfson Award.

This lay ahead. At the time, Cromwell I found to be right for me. My public grew perceptibly as I learnt to my surprise that an awful lot of people had *not* been interested in Mary Queen of Scots. And I put one cautious toe into the terrifying world of seventeenth-century English politics, where the names rung with splendour – at any rate in my ears so they rang. I would refer to my toe as dainty, by the way, except that there was nothing dainty about it. I used my historical toe, on the contrary, to blunder about in the hopes that the stately names I was encountering would give me a stately welcome.

One of the measures I embarked on was to take public speaking lessons from a friendly young woman don. She gave me an excellent tip: concentrate your mind and thus your eyes on one particular member of the audience. That will give you a rapport, which will gradually develop into an invisible alliance. It so happened that my first important speech, which took place at London University, was also particularly testing because it concerned Cromwell's intentions towards Parliament. It came in advance of the first reviews. I was ready. I picked on a surly-looking fellow with unmistakable thick hair and concentrated my words on him. My spirits lifted. In the end I felt that the applause was quite genuine.

As my young friend walked me away, she said in what I took to be an admiring manner: 'Phew! That was bold.' I smiled easily, 'You told me how to do it.'

'Yes, but to pick on *him*...' My smile became slightly less easy.

'Who was that? The one with the hair.'

She responded with the name of the leading authority on Cromwellian finances, with whom rather uppishly I had decided to disagree.

I should like to say that the story ends happily with a superb review from the expert. Unfortunately, things went in a rather different direction. I received the only really bad review of the season for that particular book.

However, not all my Cromwellian outings were quite so successful. It will not come as a surprise to sensible people to learn that the

Restoration Day, 1980, Banquet of the Royal Stuart Society. With the Governor-General. Note the Stuart props, including white roses and Bell's whisky.

Start of filming of my Jemima Shore murder mystery, *A Splash of Red*, June 1983. My cameo role lasted half a second.

Father and mother, Bernhurst, 1977.

Paddy Leigh Fermor
at Tivoli, 1974.

As Mary Queen of Scots, 1969.

The French Lieutenant's Woman
Harold discussing a shot with Karel Reisz, 1980.

Gaieties and *Guardian* cricket: Tom Stoppard and Simon Gray, 1984.

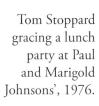

Tom Stoppard gracing a lunch party at Paul and Marigold Johnsons', 1976.

Robert De Niro
and friends, 1976.

Christmas lunch at
Campden Hill Square
with Peter Hall and
Maria Ewing, 1981.

As a French
Revolutionary at the
Austrian Embassy, 1958.

Harold
writing the
film script
for *The Trial*
in a Greek
cowshed,
early 1990s.

Harold as
the Third
Man, Paris
style.

Harold and Havel.

... and Daniel Ortega.

Orhan Pamuk, Arthur Miller and Harold, Istanbul Airport, 1985.

Patricia and Joseph Losey with Harold, 1976.

Visit to Philip Roth and
Claire Bloom at their house in
Connecticut, autumn 1984.

Harold and Oliver Sacks, 1984.

Summer 1981, party at the Stoppards'. Michael Caine holding forth.

Dinner with Jeremy Irons and friends, 1981.

Lady Antonia C.H. gives H.R.H. a history lesson, 2018.

At Campden Hill Square, with Salman Rushdie

name Oliver Cromwell attracted rather a different reaction in Ireland. However, when the time came for Hugh, my first husband, to accompany me I had somehow overlooked that. My first major outing was to Drogheda, scene of the famous siege. I was trying to identify the road that led to the original road of entry when I was lucky enough – as I saw it at the time – to catch sight of a Catholic priest standing by a small car with two nuns.

'Oh, hang on,' I said to Hugh. 'I'll just ask him the way to Cromwell's Mound…'

Off I trotted.

'Excuse me, Father, but regarding Cromwell's Mound–' At which the priest, with a look of horror, pushed the two nuns into the car, and prepared to leave precipitately himself.

'Idiot!' hissed Hugh and he walked with great politeness towards the priest, still just outside the car.

'Good morning, Father' he began, 'my wife, the daughter of the pious Lord Longford, is writing a study of the hideous assassin Oliver

Cromwell and she wondered…'

'Thataway…' said the priest with absolute calm.

Later I discovered a source of Irish folklore in a Dublin museum. The section on Cromwell opened with a question: 'Which is worse, the drink or Oliver Cromwell?' The answer was: 'The drink. Because everyone the drink kills goes to Hell, whereas everyone who Cromwell kills goes to Heaven.'

Hugh suggested I keep this answer handy in order to remember to avoid either Cromwell or the drink.

'Or Drogheda,' he added as an afterthought.

It was while I was working on Cromwell that the first serious interest in the history of English Catholicism gripped me. Events such as the Gunpowder Plot – was there finally a plot or was there not? – easily fascinated me. This was especially relevant since I had started to write detective stories in my spare time when sitting in foreign hotels, as Harold wrote or directed works of genius (as

they were laughingly known between us –
but why not?).

The determination to study the Gunpowder
Plot had the unfortunate effect of dividing
me from my U.S. publisher. She felt much
happier among the rosy clouds which, in
the popular imagination, surrounded Marie
Antoinette. But, personally, I felt I had much
more in common with some ill-fed and thus
scrawny priest, used to diving from hidey
hole to hidey hole. And I found Catholic
research in obscure archives particularly
enjoyable. As it happened my chosen parish
church in Farm Street, Mayfair, while not
exactly obscure, did have an excellent well-
arranged archive underneath the church itself
(with its altar designed by Pugin). As I have
described, there one could roam, roam with
the brain anyway, and in the intense partial
light of the subterranean room I sometimes
had the impression of taking part in a thriller
by Dan Brown.

All that I found convinced me that there
had indeed been a plot: one which was

totally justified by the civic sufferings of the Catholic people. I found myself comparing the use of violence (which I accepted had been duly planned) with Mandela's use of violence in South Africa. Everyone has some peculiar scene, small but unforgettable, in their historical imagination: mine was the moment when Mandela was released and I sat watching in my father's study (for the sake of the TV) with, as it happened, my 27-year-old son Damian. I suddenly worked it out that Mandela had been imprisoned and Damian born at roughly the same moment...

Fortunately, where Oliver Crumble was concerned, I have always had an amateurish interest in military history. Fortunately again, it is possible to combine a tour of the cricket grounds of England with an inspection of Cromwell's battlefields – which meant that Harold and I could each pursue our current interest and add to each other's pleasure. Thus, the battle of Worcester remains an interesting joint memory.

I shall never forget The Oak where Charles

II took refuge. I believe to this day that I had the honour of squatting on its royal branch, despite the rival royal branches. Harold in Heaven undoubtedly recalls the bat he bought in Worcester made out of specially (royally) treated wood.

I'm obsessed by history, says Lady Antonia

MY MOST faithful correspondent during the summer was an irate gentleman who regularly bombarded me with invective each time the Book Page carried a list of best-sellers.

The cause of his wrath was the fact that for several months Lady Antonia Fraser's biography of Mary Queen of Scots was a regular inhabitant of the lists. I do not think his objection was to the book itself as he did not appear to have read it. Rather did he address his stone towards Lady Antonia, feeling it to be an affront to decency that the work of an aristocratic amateur should be selling so well — and at four guineas a time at that.

I mention this story because it indicates the reactions of a lot of people to the news that Lady Antonia had written her book.

by
GRAHAM
LORD

LADY ANTONIA FRASER
No hangups

● IT USED to seem that Mickey Rooney would be forever young. But the fresh face did finally fade. Now he is 47 and, sadly perhaps, there are people old enough to vote today who would not recognise the features of the actor on the right, playing an innocent-teenager, helpless in the arms of an overpowering floozie — Marilyn Maxwell — in the 1948 film Summer Holiday. From THE CELLULOID MUSE, by Charles Higham and Joe Greenberg (Angus and Robertson, 50s.)

SARCASTIC

THE ANSWER

WELL TAUGHT

NO TIME

15

POLITICS AND FUN

THE EFFECT OF my upbringing was to make me think that politics was really rather fun. At least that's how I emerged from the General Election in 1945 at the age of thirteen. At that point both my parents had stood for Parliament, both Labour, neither alas successful. History was my personal passion but undoubtedly Politics was the passion of Frank and Elizabeth Pakenham, as my parents were termed until 1961.

My mother, already with six children to tend, and two more to come, Catherine and Kevin, had not stood in 1945, although she had tried her luck for Cheltenham just before the war.

Thomas and I supported her, at least that

was our story, as we attended the local school and spent most of class-time whispering fiercely:

'You tell your Mum to vote for my Mum…'

Now, my father had been created a peer, Lord Pakenham of Cowley, and joined the Labour government as a minister.

In 1961 he inherited the title of Longford from his elder brother who had no children, the name by which he is generally known today.

Personally I found electioneering highly enjoyable, and the fact that it pleased my parents to see me trotting up paths and banging on doors and putting my curly head round the door was an added benefit.

I learnt to say, in what I thought was a madly charming way: 'I'm Frank Pakenham's little girl. I hope you are going to vote for my Dada on Thursday.'

Nevertheless, it did not occur to me to write about politics – or rather elections – until I got interested in the Reform of Parliament in 1832. Suddenly, with delight, I realised that I could introduce all the little incidents which had happened to me (and my brother Thomas) as a kind of background to my serious philosophical reflections on the subject of electoral reform.

The mixture of History and Experience made working on *Perilous Question*, as my book was to be called, one of the pleasantest periods of my professional life. Once or twice in the past I had wondered … since I was so happy in my work, should I perhaps consider Parliament itself… On one occasion I found myself rushing back home and writing a long private essay headed:

Am I a Politician?

In the middle of the writing, I was summoned by my mother to make a speech to a women's organisation in the constituency where she hoped to sit.

'I'm afraid I'm too busy,' I shouted back down the stairs of our Hampstead house – we had moved from Oxford to be nearer Frank the Government Minister. 'I'm writing!' This was many years before I had become well-known as an author. But I had answered my own question. I was not a Politician. I was a Writer.

At Cliveden in 1958; Atalanta and Richard Fairey
arriving in style.

16

FUN AGAIN

I NEVER EXPECTED to use my canvassing
skills again – and certainly not for the
Tories. But my happy marriage in 1956 to
an established and popular Tory MP, when
he was nearly forty and I was twenty-three,
meant just that. Only now I was Mr Fraser's
smiling girl rather than Mr Pakenham's.

The real excitement of my new life was
not so much in the constituency as in the
House of Commons – meaning of course
the ladies' gallery. I shall never forget the
first day I sat there – alone of course as Hugh
was somewhere below and I had no idle girl
friends who would leave their jobs at my
command.

Suddenly there was an extraordinary long,

low, growling sound, actually men's voices. Grrr, grr, grrrr, rrrrr... I peered into the huge chamber below in amazement. Only to see a tiny toad-like figure crawling, as it seemed, along the path between the two sides of MPs below us. The tiny figure was being greeted, yes, it was, it was being cheered...

Grrr, grr, grr ... oh heavens! It was Mr Churchill.

There he was, although no longer Prime Minister. My hero! The voice of courage coming from the darkness of the wartime radio... Once again I was eight years old, praying for Mr Churchill. 'Dear God, please look after our noble leader...'

Altogether I enjoyed being the wife of an MP very much. There were the dramas (after all, history cannot hold on to all the dramas).

Hugh yawned at one breakfast time and indicated that there had been some kerfuffle in the Commons, a kerfuffle not yet resolved. I was only half listening. Some MP had denied an affair with some damsel or something like that.

I do remember asking Hugh: 'Did he do it?' without being particularly interested in the answer. Which was:

'Of course he did it.' A pause. Then: 'Everyone has always done it.'

So began the Profumo Case, which was to haunt British politics. I muttered something like: 'Jack Profumo is a charming man' – true – and passed on. Within quite a short space of time nobody talked about anything else. Jack Profumo *was* charming, and so for that matter was his wife, the lovely actress Valerie Hobson: she had acted with special benevolence when I took her into Wandsworth Prison to take part in a showbiz quiz in aid of a prison charity. There were two fairly large panels – but such was Valerie's amusing sweetness that no one really wanted to talk to anyone else.

In the course of time the attitude of society to the Profumos became less honeyed. Hugh and I, who continued to like and even admire them both, were able to do Jack a good turn by introducing him to my father.

From my father to Toynbee Hall was a short leap: Jack went to work there and once again charmed the world with his industry and his imagination.

In short, politics was fun if you vaguely hoped to serve your country and, in the process, did nothing of which the *Daily Express* might joyfully disapprove.

17

THE WEDDING
FEAST

'SIXTY YEARS,' SAID Frances Pinter proudly. 'We have been married sixty years next week. Buckingham Palace is interested.' On examination this turned out to be something to do with a telegram of congratulation. There seemed to be an idea that it was the role of the daughter-in-law to secure it.

Once I had understood what was wanted, I was happy to grab the telephone book and ring up Buckingham Palace. And I was very civilly received, just a quick polite question: 'You are quite sure it is sixty years since Mr and Mrs Pinter got married? The nicest old people can be a little vague…'

Luckily, exactly the same point had struck me. I had already delicately enquired, and been rewarded by the sight of a treasured wedding certificate pulled out of a carefully locked drawer. No doubt at all about it. Sixty years before Frances and Jack had tied the knot.

I began to plan for a splendid lunch party in our Notting Hill house to which the Pinters would be brought from their long-term residence in Hove. Here Harold, their only child, retired them when he wrote *The Caretaker* and enjoyed his first flush of cash. I liked all their friends; my cleaning lady was delighted to masquerade as a butler; what could go wrong?

For example, had I not managed to get us married avoiding the date of Yom Kippur? Admittedly this had needed a little help from Frances. She had taken me aside when Harold's divorce was finally through and said that she was going to ask a great favour. This turned out to be:

Do not get married on Yom Kippur (the Day of the Dead in the Jewish religion). Hastily but ardently I absolutely promised not to get married on any such date. Secretly I asked Harold why on earth she had made such an extraordinary request.

'Oh, because Vivien and I did get married on Yom Kippur,' he replied carelessly. 'Neither of us realised.' By now I was sufficiently invested in the awesome day to be absolutely horrified. I resolved all over again it should not happen twice.

I bought diaries from America as being more reliable and finally settled on absolutely the right day.

At which point Harold blew my happiness apart.

'What about the food? It must of course be Kosher…'

Every time we went to Hove and had lunch with the Pinters I made a mental note about the food. I watched Frances and noted that she never touched shellfish. That was easy to remember. I also grabbed Jack's copy of the *Jewish Chronicle* whenever I found it lying about and picked up tips. But none of that amounted to sufficient intelligence to create a planned Kosher menu, which I could compare only to Catholic Lent, avoiding forbidden fruit – except, of course, Lent lasts only forty days.

When, rather nervously, I asked Frances' kind friend Ruth, who also lived in Hove, about the sort of menu I should provide, she suggested I should take some sort of Jewish cooking course. I muttered something about being busy with my biography of Oliver Cromwell (who happened to be an admirer of the Jews). It seemed as good an excuse as any for not getting the food absolutely right.

I was reckoning without God. Such a mistake.

Exactly a month before my projected celebration lunch I received an unprecedented invitation. What was more, it concerned me only, Harold was not included. Yet it was to lunch at Kensington Palace… The answer was that Shimon Peres, Prime Minister of Israel, would be there. And he was a historian. So, historians – not husbands and wives – were asked to meet him. (I had in fact briefly met him during my sole, never-to-be-forgotten visit to Israel.) The Prince and Princess of Wales, neither of whom I had ever met before, were the hosts.

I was completely confident that a combination of God, the Princess of Wales and the Royal Housekeeper would provide a Kosher menu. I sank to my knees in a rush of gratitude.

The great day came. Unfortunately, I set out about half an hour early, I simply could not help it. That meant some rather tedious time lurking in the park, as it doesn't take long to get from Campden Hill Square to Kensington Palace. I was rewarded by the utterly graceful sight of Princess Diana swooping into her drawing room and chatting up the Israeli Ambassador. She was clutching her little boy, Prince William. Conversation was sweetness itself.

'Is it hot in Israel? Oh, I do hope it's hot. I long for a hot weather holiday… ' And so on.

NOW to the food.

'I've got a photographic memory. I have. I know I have,' I told myself. All I needed to do was take an image of the table with my agile brain. The only problem was the contents of the food. A photograph in the brain didn't always tell you how to make it with your hands. All the same, I left with an indelible image of chicken. A special kind of Israeli chicken.

So, thank you God for that unexpected rescue. There was only one oddity: at the long-planned lunch my special chicken dish seemed to present a mystery to everyone there. Nobody piped up to say: 'Oh we *always* had this on my birthday,' for example.

And finally, daring Ruthie asked: 'What is this lovely food?'

Last time God … this time Harold.

'Oh, this is Antonia's speciality,' he said. 'We call it Chicken Antoinette.' Silence fell, broken by a muttered protest from Jack Pinter. He was just beginning to say: 'I've never heard of it,' when Frances Pinter spoke up. She didn't often speak but when she did it was always to the point.

'My mother adored this chicken,' she said – just audibly – as she munched.

First God, then Harold, finally Frances. I was very lucky on that day, the sixtieth anniversary of my parents-in-law's wedding.

18

SQUISH

My NEW PASSION for libraries got off to a slightly shaky start. Hugh had been asked to shoot at Chatsworth and generously decided that I couldn't be left behind for the weekend. Andrew Devonshire equally generously decided that I should be included in the guest list, even though it was dominated by the Prime Minister Harold Macmillan, a keen shot at all times and related to the family by marriage (he had married Andrew's aunt, Lady Dorothy Cavendish).

'Hooray!' I cried. 'I can work in the library. Mary Queen of Scots…' and my voice trailed away as I realised no one was listening, and probably never would really listen so long as the MQS phrase hovered above the conversation.

So, the shoot progressed until lunch time and then we all adjourned to the school house, or anyway some similarly modest but comfortable building.

'Well, I'm off to the library,' I said in a falsely jolly voice.

There was silence for a moment ... then another moment. Then Macmillan's unmistakable voice was heard.

'Thomas Hobbes, who was librarian to the then Earl of Devonshire, said: "Libraries, my lord, do more harm than good, for they set fools a-wondering."'

Squish. Definitely squish.

With George Weidenfeld, 1990.

19

GOOD CHEER

Long before George Weidenfeld flashed his ambitious green eyes in my direction and pointed to bestselling books, shovelling them in my direction, my mother encouraged all her children to write.

This was symbolised for me by letter writing at Christmas. On the one hand we had to write to our uncles and aunts and politely ask them for what my mother had already bought for us. On the other hand – much more exciting – we had to write to Father Christmas himself and demand the globe. Or anyway a little piece of it. And Father Christmas was watching. Wasn't he?

Everyone had to believe in Father Christmas – otherwise no tree, no presents, no elegant gentleman from unknown foreign parts striding into the drawing room on Christmas afternoon, dragging a sack or even two sacks, in short no real Christmas. You just HAD to believe.

That was why the night of the Tartan Trousers was so dangerous. I ran the risk of blowing the great man back up his chimney and on some cloud, away, away… After all, hadn't our mother told us that the only thing we must always do is believe in Father Christmas?

Finally, each year we did reach Boxing Day.

'Christmas comes but once a year,' my mother was apt to sing out on Boxing Day, 'but when it comes it brings good cheer.' We children – eight of us by the end – exchanged meaningful glances.

Then Thomas, ever enquiring, spoke up: 'Will Father Christmas come back next year?' Judith was more probing: 'Where does he live all the rest of the year?' Since this was 1945 and my father was due to stand for Parliament in the coming summer General

Election – in the Labour interest in Oxford – I thought it tactful to ask: 'Will he vote Labour?'

My mother did not seem to like the political question very much. 'Of course he will vote Labour,' she snapped, 'and bring us a lot of good things just like Labour will.'

I saw my chance: 'But if he comes but once a year, that's not very much, is it?' I added: 'I'd really rather have something more regular, like a van which comes by. You'd know it was Father Christmas by his red jacket with the white fur and the funny hood.'

'Doesn't Father Christmas have any other clothes? What about summertime?' It was Thomas as usual, trying to ask an awkward question. Then we all went on our separate ways, grumbling about Father Christmas, except me who was in a romantic phase and wondered if he was tall and dark and handsome, or just tall, like a deer.

That year a very peculiar thing happened in our house, which seemed in a bizarre fashion to answer Thomas' question. Our Uncle John arrived for Christmas: he was our mother's unmarried brother (he later went on to marry, and became the father of the distinguished Labour politician Harriet Harman). He tended to sleep in a bachelor bedroom in the attic. I happened to be rooting about there, no doubt seeing if I could add to my own presents in advance, when I heard familiar voices: our mother and Uncle John.

'They won't show,' said our mother.

'It's important,' said the voice of Uncle John. He seemed to be wrestling with something.

Then I fled and began wrapping my presents for the next day. But I managed to leave a vital object upstairs, and it was in that way, another secret creep, that I came on a garish pair of tartan trousers lying half-hidden by his bed. And imagine my amazement when the next day, as Father Christmas danced in the drawing room, to see, clearly visible, another pair of garish trousers, beneath his scarlet robe. Another pair? Surely it must be the same pair … but that was impossible.

How would Uncle John manage to get hold of Father Christmas' trousers?

I decided to find out by cunning questioning.

'Do you know Scotland, Uncle John?' I asked in a voice of casual politeness. (I was rather proud of that voice.) 'No!' he said firmly. That was a bit of a facer. 'What about tartan?' I persisted. 'No, I can't bear tartan.' In a way that was a tremendous relief: I loved my romantic notion of the secret donor, and anyway our visitor had been quite tall, and quite dark and very handsome. Father Christmas was real.

'Christmas comes but once a year,' declared my mother at the end of the year in a proud voice. 'And next year it's going to provide more cheer than ever. Your father and I have bought a little cottage in Scotland... The only thing is that the Scots don't really celebrate Christmas. It's New Year up there.'

'New Year!' I cried with horror. 'But what about Father Christmas?'

'Oh, Father Christmas is coming too,' said

Uncle John casually. 'A real opportunity to wear my new trousers. I love dressing up and Christmas is the perfect opportunity. Did you think they suited me?'

Horrors! Father Christmas really was just playing a game. I muttered to myself: 'When Christmas comes it brings a tear...' And I was beginning to decide that Uncle John's Trousers stood for all that was false in life. At which point there was a shout from my mother.

'Antonia,' she hallooed. 'There's an invitation for you. Do you remember Lord Weidenfeld? He runs a new exciting publisher. And he wants a young woman to go and work there.'

And the rest was (more or less) History.

Caroline Lamb and Caroline Norton.

20

SWEET CAROLINES

AT THE BEGINNING of the twenty-first century my stars must have been twinkling in some delightful arrangement celebrating the name Caroline. Because in the first quarter I spent an extraordinary and extraordinarily happy time dealing with two fascinating women by that name. I should have been proud to have called either of them Sister.

Caroline Norton and Caroline Lamb (the order in which I wrote their biographies, although Caroline Norton was born in 1808 and Caroline Lamb in 1785) had one tremendous connection, and that was through William Lamb, Lord Melbourne. Lady Caroline Lamb was married to him at the age of nineteen, although it should be noted that William succeeded his father to the Melbourne title only after her death, so that she never bore the Melbourne name. Caroline Norton was accused of adultery with William Lamb, by now Lord Melbourne, by her husband George Norton.

In fact, I reached the decision to write about Caroline Norton through quite a different route. I was attracted by the law case, which involved the alleged offence she had committed with Melbourne. The law had always attracted me – wistfully I had sometimes dreamt of it as a profession and had to be content to have it pointed out in kindly fashion by the various distinguished lawyers in my family that a biographer was a kind of barrister. Furthermore, Caroline's law case ended in a terrible way, with the removal of her three children from their mother's care.

The boys were sent to a relation in Scotland. There, the youngest, nine-year-old Willy, fell mortally ill as a result of a riding accident.

Caroline Norton was summoned back into the family circle. Too late. She was met at the station by a certain Lady Kelly, whom she had never met before.

'How's Willy?' she asked.

'Dead' was the brief cruel answer.

In short, the story of Caroline Norton became one of the struggle for the rights of the mother, which scarcely existed at the time. I loved writing about the case, alternately shedding inner tears over the fate of Willy (imagine that scene on the railway platform) and exploding with indignation over the behaviour of George Norton. It was a great story to write, for just these reasons. Caroline Norton could not exactly be described as a feminist – living as she did in the age of early feminist advances – but the delineation of her attitude towards women's rights was a fascinating study.

She herself, one of three beautiful Sheridan sisters, made for marvellous illustrations.

If a biographer can have a tiny secret self-identification with the subject, I definitely felt something along those lines for Caroline Norton: not so much 'that happened to me' as 'how terrible if that HAD happened to me.' With Caroline Lamb, I had never harboured any intention of writing about her, one Caroline being sweet enough, until the spiritual darkness of Lockdown. In a melancholy fashion I was dusting where no duster had ever been before. Suddenly a large book fell deliberately – as I perceived it – on my foot. It was not a book that I had con-sciously read or bought. It was a biography. But Lady Caroline Lamb or L C L* was there for me. I could take the hint.

One night I acquired the film featuring Sarah Miles as L C L on Amazon and watched it with my daughter Natasha. We both adored Sarah Miles in the character of

---

* Lady Caroline Lamb became known in the family as L C L for the obvious reason of avoiding confusion with Caroline Norton. Especially since the life of Caroline Norton – *The Case of the Married Woman* – was my previous title and still hanging around bookshops. The song 'Sweet Caroline' by Neil Diamond came naturally to the lips.

Caroline, while disapproving of the actor playing Byron, whose name I have tactfully forgotten. There was an irresistible comparison between the two Carolines, suffused by a kind of tender wonder at the mad courage on show.

For L C L I had mixed emotions; but whatever my irritation, shared by Lady Melbourne and no doubt at times by Byron himself, I always felt a kind of tenderness, a wish to take the naughty little creature under my wing, which I had never felt before with any of my subjects (and this was a list which included not one but four executions!).

In this way I secured to myself five very happy years, writing about the Sweeties. I found myself telling a romantic story in both cases: and in both cases centred on William Lamb, aka Lord Melbourne, although there were plenty of other men of many different sorts involved. Not only that: there are plenty of romantic stories in women's history, but the stories of the fight for women's rights were more limited and therefore in a way more exciting.

When it came to women's rights, L C L presented a very different attitude from Caroline Norton. Where the latter campaigned with energy and intelligence, contributing a great deal to the whole female picture including matters like divorce as well as the vital mother's rights, L C L took action – often quite dramatic action. The following was typical of Caroline Lamb: when her beloved William was about to make his first speech as an MP in the House of Commons, she found to her horror that women were not admitted. What did Caroline Lamb do? She dressed up as a boy with the help of her brother's clothes and proceeded to attend in style.

It became rapidly apparent that, rather than look like a man, Caroline Lamb wanted to enjoy a man's liberties and freedoms.

I was writing at a time of feverish transgender discussions and even contemporary actions. L C L taught me that the fight for liberty can take many forms, including that of a sprightly page. As I gaze at my reproduction of Caroline the page by Thomas Philips (commissioned by L C L's cousin the Duke of Devonshire, and now at Chatsworth) I reflect on what a delightful government minister she would have made today.

H.M. meets H.P.

21

SHE WAS OUR
QUEEN

The Corgi's Lament

When a soft white hand
Caressed my fur
I knew it was her
When a gentle slap
Discouraged my yap
I knew it was her
I'll miss the caress
I'll miss the slap
Most of all
The Royal Shoes
Planted so near
Planted so long

In charge of my fate
Shining and strong
Her dogs, her dears
She calmed our fears
We knew from those Shoes
That we can't bear to lose
She was our Queen

I wrote this in a burst of passion, stirred by the Poet Laureate in *The Times*. I had spent most of the previous week, it seemed, waiting for the Queen to die. Son Benjie invited me to his favourite club, 5 Hertford Street, and, as the news of her health flickered to and fro, we formed a tiny special bond. As a result, we decided to spend the day of the funeral together, in the hospitable drawing room of 52 Campden Hill Square, watching television.

There was a pause when the royal coffin departed by train for Windsor.

Benjie stood up.

'I shall cook lunch,' he said. Such a thing had never been said before by Benjie anywhere near my kitchen. It seemed a suitable tribute to Her Majesty, similar to my own little Verse.

Royal Wedding commentary, 1981, with
David Frost.

22

THE DUCHESS

I BECAME A monarchist when I was very young, reading Henrietta Marshall's *Our Island Story*. Actually 'monarchist' was not quite accurate. It was Princesses (and possibly Princes) that interested me, but even I faltered at the idea of being a Princess. Or did I? With the lovely Queen gone, I began to take an interest in Kate, Princess of Wales, for her intelligence even before her beauty. And then there was Meghan, Duchess of Sussex… Surely she was being harshly treated, like many eccentric characters in History?

I decided to write to the Duchess a friendly letter of welcome as a historian of women: 'there has always been a place for the individual woman who knows her own mind…'

I checked the royal address with care. Then, out of decency, bearing in mind the huge post she must receive, I finished the letter: 'No need to reply.'

And she didn't. Time passed. I forgot about my letter and forgot too about the Duchess herself.

Some four months later my letter was returned to me: 'Not Known at This Address'.

23

HUT 'N HISTORY

I CAN'T HELP ending on the (to me) ever-exciting topic of Myself and History. Naturally the way we write and what we write are heavily influenced by our personal circumstances. You try to suppress those feelings but, as with any work of art, find it impossible. The political situation in England when I was writing a certain chapter in Cromwell's life was such that inevitably it got reflected in my book. I remember throwing the *Daily Telegraph* across the room and shouting 'Take that, Old Noll' before calmer counsels prevailed.

Having admitted that, the whole question of personal involvement and how much it warps historical judgements is a fascinating one. I fell in love with Scotland the first moment I was introduced to the Fraser house which was to be mine. Eilean Aigas, as its name (eilean = island) indicates, lies placidly in the middle of the rushing Beauly river. Thanks to the success of *Mary Queen of Scots* I was able to introduce Highland delights such as a tennis court and swimming pool. And on the banks of the river I introduced My Hut.

How did I choose where to build the Hut? I invited my son Damian, then seven, to answer the telephone travelling as far as he could be reasonably bothered (this was of course long before the days of portable telephones: Eilean Aigas had a single battered instrument in what was known as the Book Room). As it was, I wrote the whole of my short life of King James VI and I, sitting in my Hut, over one weekend.

In fact, I think if I could live my life again, I would find myself in my Hut writing History.

1962.

EPILOGUE

I WAS THERE

AT THE END of my long life I find that I really love History. The squeamish wriggles I used to have about mediaeval history were gone – how could I interest myself in the White Ship yet again and come up with some lyrical prose? Answer, in a sharp voice: you didn't write lyrical prose the first time so why not face it? It is just not your area of expertise.

I feel free to enjoy History in all its different aspects, diving here, diving there, emerging somewhere quite different. I also feel oddly proud of having lived through certain historical periods, such as the Blitz in London (I used to visit a weekly doctor there) without having in any way contributed anything significant to them. It was like walking on the tower of Bodiam Castle. I was there.

In fact, 'I was there' was my secret motto as a Historian. If I can imagine that I was there, then I have a sporting chance of conveying the same excitement to my readers. And even if not, I was there: I walked with Mary Queen of Scots, I hid out with Charles II, I bowed before Marie Antoinette and wept at her grave... I was there.

Acknowledgements

A LIFETIME SPENT in books leaves me thankful to a great many people – as well as a great many books. Principal among them is the publisher of *Patchwork Pieces*, Sam Carter; our association began with the publication of *My Ethiopian Diary*. Then there was the wonderful publisher of so much of my work, Alan Samson, who urged me on in this project. My family, especially Flora Fraser, has as ever been quizzically encouraging, and my dear agent, Jonathan Lloyd, always came when called, whilst Rozzy organised things at home. Harry Mount did me the honour of printing extracts in *The Oldie*. The book is dedicated to the late Tristram Powell, with whom I so often discussed these topics, half in wisdom, half in laughter.